D1507755

Merry Christmas + Happy New Year

Ernie

ISBN 1-58660-874-6

Cover image © GettyOne

Scripture quotations marked KJV are taken from the King James Version of the Bible.

Scripture quotations marked NIV are taken from the HOLY BIBLE, NEW INTERNATIONAL VERSION®. NIV®. Copyright © 1973, 1978, 1984 by International Bible Society. Used by permission of Zondervan Publishing House. All rights reserved.

Scripture quotations marked NKJV are taken from the New King James Version. Copyright © 1979, 1980, 1982 by Thomas Nelson, Inc. Used by permission. All rights reserved.

Scripture quotations marked CEV are from the Contemporary English Version © 1991, 1992, 1995 by American Bible Society. Used by permission.

Selections by Pamela Rowell, Ruth Gillett, and Pamela Dowd, used by permission.

Published by Barbour Publishing, Inc., P.O. Box 719, Uhrichsville, Ohio 44683, www.barbourbooks.com

Member of the
Evangelical Christian
Publishers Association

Printed in China.
5 4 3 2 1

STAR OF Wonder

VICKIE PHELPS

DayMaker
GREETING BOOKS

A Christmas Prayer

May the Christmas star be your constant guide
this season. May its message give you
comfort in the midst of chaos.
May its radiating light lead you to
the Prince of Peace.

O star of wonder, star of light,
Star with royal beauty bright,
Westward leading, still proceeding,
Guide us to thy perfect light.

JOHN H. HOPKINS, JR.

When they had heard the king, they departed; and, lo, the star, which they saw in the east, went before them, till it came and stood over where the young child was. When they saw the star, they rejoiced with exceeding great joy.

MATTHEW 2:9–10 KJV

And suddenly there was with the angel
a multitude of the heavenly host praising God,
and saying, Glory to God in the highest,
and on earth peace, good will toward men.

LUKE 2:13–14 KJV

In the hectic flurry of holiday activities,
the angel's message can easily be lost.
In an effort to celebrate to the fullest,
we sometimes place unrealistic demands on
ourselves. When the season comes to an end,
we may realize we have not celebrated peace,
but rather buried it beneath a mountain of
obligations. During this season of peace and
goodwill, may we remember the news
proclaimed so joyously on that night
centuries ago: "Glory to God in the highest,
and on earth peace,
good will toward men."

In the darkest night the star did shine,
Proclaiming the Savior's birth.
And wise men today who trust His name
Still proclaim the Savior on earth.

PAMELA F. DOWD

I heard the bells on Christmas day
Their old familiar carols play,
And wild and sweet
The words repeat
Of peace on earth, goodwill to men!

And in despair I bowed my head;
"There is no peace on earth," I said;
"For hate is strong
And mocks the song
Of peace on earth, goodwill to men!"

Then pealed the bells more loud and deep,
"God is not dead; nor doth He sleep!
The wrong shall fail,
The right prevail,
With peace on earth, goodwill to men!"

HENRY WADSWORTH LONGFELLOW

* * * * * *

"For my eyes
have seen your salvation,
which you prepared
in the sight of all people."

LUKE 2:30–31 NIV

Peace is like. . .

- a gentle dove arriving on quiet wing with its soothing message.
- a bubbling brook which flows unmindful over the obstacles in its path.
- a soft breeze that caresses and refreshes our spirit.

$\mathcal{H}$ave you ever spent an anxious, sleepless night, tossing and turning in frustration, wishing for morning and the peace it would bring? In my Bible reading one day, I discovered Psalm 4:8: "I will both lay me down in peace, and sleep: for thou, LORD, only makest me dwell in safety" (KJV). On those nights when sleep evades me or anxiety keeps me disturbed, the message of this verse brings me peace and sleep follows soon after.

* * * * * *

My precious little angel,

With eyes so sweet and bright,

Sleep in peace my darling,

Jesus Christ was born tonight.

PAMELA F. DOWD

God

takes care of his own,

even while they sleep.

PSALM 127:2 CEV

Mary must have suffered some anxiety as she awaited the birth of her son. Joseph, too, may have wondered what the future held for his family. But the star that came to rest over the place where the Christ child lay brought a message of its own. It led visitors to Bethlehem—visitors who worshiped the babe. Surely this confirmation brought peace to Mary and Joseph that this was a holy night, and the child was indeed, the Prince of Peace.

Silent night! Holy night!
All is calm, All is bright,
Round yon Virgin, Mother and Child,
Holy Infant, so tender and mild,
Sleep in heavenly peace,
Sleep in heavenly peace.

JOSEF MOHR

A crash interrupted "Silent Night" and made the heart of the harried mother sink. "Why can't I have one moment of peace?"

She hurried to reprimand the culprit. "Nathan!"

He stood by the nativity scene where a broken lamb lay beside the manger. He held up a dust cloth in stubby, toddler fingers, tears dripping down his chin. "I was. . ."

Her anger fizzled. He'd been helping. Her heart felt at peace as she took both the cloth and the little hand, guiding him to dry the tears and clean the mess. *How many times,* she wondered, *has Jesus dried my tears and erased the evidence of my failures?*

She hugged her son to her as she realized in the midst of the season, she'd been looking for peace in her circumstances and lost sight of the Prince of Peace.

PAMELA ROWELL

May the silent night fill your holidays
with quiet reflection.
May the calm surrender
of the baby fill your life with peace.
May you find all the blessings
the Savior came to share.

PAMELA F. DOWD

"My soul magnifies the Lord,
and my spirit has rejoiced
in God my Savior."

LUKE 1:46–47 NKJV

May you have
the gladness of Christmas which is hope;
the spirit of Christmas which is peace;
the heart of Christmas which is love.

AVA V. HENDRICKS

No Peace without Jesus

World leaders sit in high places.
Tired eyes, distress on their faces.
Before them their agenda folders,
The weight of world peace upon their shoulders.

The leader stood, addressed the crowd.
"World peace is our plan," he spoke out loud.
"We've stockpiled arms; we've picked the men;
We'll stop the fighting this time again!"

The crowd cheered. He'd voiced their resolve,
No thought of the pain this would involve.
An old man stood and quelled the cheers.
"Are our hearts so cold our ears can't hear?"

"Are our minds so vain our mouths can't cease?
We'll not succeed in bringing world peace.
Peace comes when the Babe of Bethlehem reigns,
No peace without Christ, the balm for our pain!"

RUTH GILLETT

When my heart
is at peace,
the world is at peace.

CHINESE PROVERB

Where there is faith,
there is love;
Where there is love,
there is peace;
Where there is peace,
there is God;
And where there is God;
there is no need.

LEO TOLSTOY

With all the hustle and bustle
associated with the holidays, would
we even hear the angels if they
were singing o'er our heads?

PAMELA ROWELL

There is but one way
to tranquility of mind and happiness,
and that is to account no external things
thine own, but to commit all to God.

EPICTETUS

While looking through a box of old holiday photos, I studied the facial expressions of friends and family. In one picture, three ladies sat on the floor, one smiling; one solemn; the other with her eyes closed against the flash. The camera captured yawning faces, surprised faces, and even a few tired faces. But the overriding expression on young and old alike was peace. I noticed how we had changed as we grew older; hairlines had receded, weight fluctuated, and gray strands of hair replaced dark ones, but still we exhibited peace. It came into each of our lives through Christ. The same peace still exists for those who seek it.

*I*t came upon the midnight clear,
That glorious song of old.
From angels bending near the earth
To touch their harps of gold!
"Peace on the earth, good will to men,
From heaven's all gracious King!"
The world in solemn stillness lay
To hear the angels sing.

EDMUND H. SEARS

*I*magine the joy of the Father
as he looked at his newborn Son.
It must have lit all heaven with praise
to see what the Heavenly Father had done.
The angels joined their voices
with the heavenly throng,
Until their laughter filled the
air with joy and jubilant song!
And those on earth in one small
realm could only guess the joy
As Mary and Joseph held the
hand of God's redeeming boy.
We too can join the celestial
chorus that began so long ago
As we embrace the Father's Son
sent from heaven to earth below.

PAMELA F. DOWD

"You will go out in joy
and be led forth in peace."

ISAIAH 55:12 NIV

These things I have spoken unto you,
that in me ye might have peace.
In the world ye shall have
tribulation: but be of good cheer;
I have overcome the world.

JOHN 16:33 KJV

How comforting to serve a God who wants to give us peace. His Word assures that He speaks to us for that reason. Even though we may have problems, He encourages us to be of good cheer. He is the bearer of good tidings, bringing us comfort and joy.

*G*od rest you merry, gentlemen,
Let nothing you dismay,
Remember Christ our Savior
Was born on Christmas Day,
To save us all from Satan's power
When we were gone astray:
O tidings of comfort and joy,
   comfort and joy,
O tidings of comfort and joy.

TRADITIONAL ENGLISH CAROL

$\mathcal{G}od's$ peace can come at any time. It's not limited to good times or calendar days. No watch controls it; no man can change it; no enemy can take it from you. You can experience God's magnificent gift of peace at anytime during the year. But what better time to receive this gift than during the season of peace on earth, goodwill to men.

Peace is. . .

- gazing at the stars with the knowledge that you know their Creator.

- closing your eyes in sleep without fear of tomorrow.

- the stillness in your heart when trouble swirls around you.

- a quiet mind in a raging world.

F or unto us a child is born, unto us a son
is given: and the government shall be upon
his shoulder: and his name shall be called
Wonderful, Counsellor, The mighty God,
The everlasting Father, The Prince of Peace.

ISAIAH 9:6 KJV

* * * * * *

A Christmas Prayer for You

May the peace of the Christ child fill your
mind and spirit, shutting out the frustration
and anxiety brought on by a world in turmoil.
May you have the mind of Christ as you
celebrate His birth.

And the peace of God, which passeth all
understanding, shall keep your hearts and
minds through Christ Jesus.

PHILIPPIANS 4:7 KJV

God sent a star to light the night
for The Way, The Truth, The Life—His Son.
He sent the Light of Life to prove His heart
so we would invite His Son into our own.
God has given us all the light we'll ever
need to find peace on earth, goodwill to men.

PAMELA F. DOWD

"*I* am the light of the world.
He who follows Me shall not walk in darkness,
but have the light of life."

JOHN 8:12 NKJV

* * * * * *

The peace of Christmas is not. . .

- presents piled under a decorated tree.
- a table loaded with food.
- a charge card pushed to the limit.
- the company party.
- more lights than anyone else in the neighborhood.
- giving a more expensive gift.

The peace of Christmas is. . .

- hearing again the story of Christ's birth.
- singing age-old carols you believe in.
- watching children perform the nativity story.
- being in the company of those you love.
- realizing that all the trappings are nice, but not necessary.
- knowing the Christ of Christmas is a reality every day.

Voices in the Mist

The time draws near the birth of Christ.
The moon is hid, the night is still.
The Christmas bells from hill to hill
Answer each other in the mist.

Four voices of four hamlets round,
From far and near, on mead and moor,
Swell out and fail, as if a door
Were shut before me and the sound:

Each voice four changes on the wind,
That now dilate, and note decrease,
Peace and goodwill, goodwill and peace,
Peace and goodwill, to all mankind.

ALFRED TENNYSON

*G*reat peace have they which love
thy law: and nothing shall offend them.

PSALM 119:165 KJV

* * * * * *

*B*lessed are the peacemakers:
for they shall be called
the children of God.

MATTHEW 5:9 KJV

For Christ is born of Mary,
And gathered all above,
While mortals sleep, the angels keep
Their watch of wondering love.
O morning stars, together
Proclaim the holy birth!
And praises sing to God the King,
And peace to men on earth.

PHILLIPS BROOKS